RUBANK
Treasures
for FRENCH HORN

ONLINE MEDIA INCLUDED
Audio Recordings
Printable Piano Accompaniments

PLAYBACK+
Speed • Pitch • Balance • Loop

CONTENTS

To access recordings and PDF piano accompaniments, go to:
www.halleonard.com/mylibrary
Enter Code
4884-6635-9312-8264

ISBN 978-1-4803-5250-6

RUBANK®

HAL•LEONARD®
7777 W. BLUEMOUND RD. P.O. BOX 13819 MILWAUKEE, WI 53213

Visit Hal Leonard Online at
www.halleonard.com

Andante Cantabile

French Horn

Guiseppe Tartini
Transcribed by H. Voxman

0121442

American Patrol

French Horn

F. W. Meacham
Arranged by Herman A. Hummel

Starling

French Horn

Hale A. VanderCook

0121442

Pavane pour une Infante Défunte

French Horn

Maurice Ravel
Arranged by Clarence E. Hurrell

00121442

In the Hall of the Mountain King

from *Peer Gynt Suite*

French Horn

Edvard Grieg
Arranged by G. E. Holmes

Marcia marcato (♩ = 96)

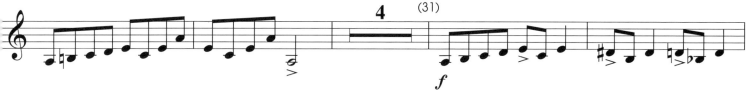

Heroica

8

French Horn

E. DeLamater

00121442

Ballade

French Horn

Vyacheslav Shchyolokov
(V. Shelukov)
Edited by William Gower

00121442

Where'er You Walk

from *Semele*

French Horn

G. F. Handel
Arranged by Clair W. Johnson

00121442

Après un Rêve

(After a Dream)

French Horn

Gabriel Fauré
Transcribed by H. Voxman

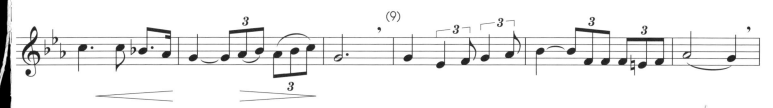

00121442

Toreador's Song
from *Carmen*

French Horn

Georges Bizet
Arranged by G. E. Holmes

Allegro moderato (♩ = 116)

Sérénade

(Sing, Smile, Slumber)

French Horn

Charles Gounod
Arranged by G. E. Holmes

Moderato (♩. = 63)

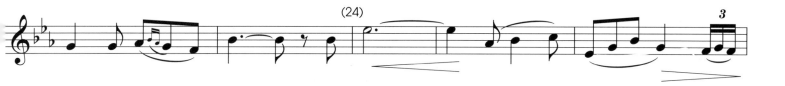

00121442

Serenade
Op. 22, No. 1

French Horn

Oskar Böhme
Edited by H. Voxman

Tempo I

Più lento (♩ = 88)

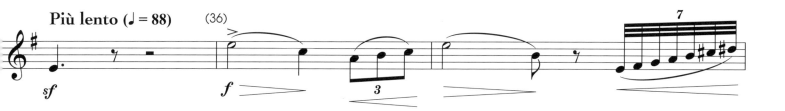

Più vivo (♩ = 120)

16

Air Gai

French Horn

G. P. Berlioz
Edited by H. Voxman

00121442

Alleluja

from *Exsultate, Jubilate, K. 165*

French Horn

W. A. Mozart
Arranged by Clair W. Johnson

Prelude and Fanfaronade

French Horn

Paul Koepke

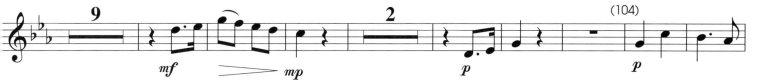

HAL LEONARD
SOLO AND ENSEMBLE SERIES

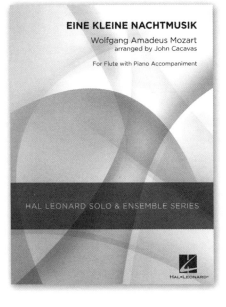

EINE KLEINE NACHTMUSIK
Wolfgang Amadeus Mozart
arranged by John Cacavas

For Flute with Piano Accompaniment

HAL LEONARD SOLO & ENSEMBLE SERIES

The Hal Leonard Solo and Ensemble Series is the perfect solution for elementary to intermediate level students looking for great solo material!

- Features classic and original solo literature for grades 1.5 to 3
- Sure to become staples on every state contest and festival list
- Each includes piano accompaniment
- Retails for only $5.99 each!

HAL•LEONARD®

FLUTE
04002802	**Overture to *The Barber of Seville*** (Puccini) Gr. 3
04002803	**Eine Kleine Nachtmusik** (Mozart) Gr. 3
04002804	**Minuet – Rondo** (Loeillet) Gr. 2.5
04002805	**Poem** (Cacavas) Gr. 2.5

CLARINET
04002814	**Allemande and Courante** (Froberger) Gr. 3
04002815	**Harlequin Dance** (Cacavas) Gr. 2
04002816	**Impressionistic Air** (Cacavas) Gr. 2
04002817	**Theme from Symphony No. 40** (Beethoven) Gr. 3

OBOE
04002806	**Danse Ancienne** (Cacavas) Gr. 2
04002807	**Theme from Symphony No. 40** (Mozart) Gr. 3
04002808	**Minuet and Trio** (Bach) Gr. 2.5
04002809	**Summer Pastiche** (Cacavas) Gr. 2.5

BASSOON
04002810	**Liebestraum** (Liszt) Gr. 2
04002811	**Minuet and Trio** (Bach) Gr. 2.5
04002812	**Poem** (Cacavas) Gr. 3
04002813	**Sonatina** (Weber) Gr. 3

ALTO SAXOPHONE
04002818	**Harlequin Dance** (Cacavas) Gr. 2
04002819	**Minuet – Rondo** (Loeillet) Gr. 2.5
04002820	**Minuet and Trio** (Bach) Gr. 2.5
04002821	**Summer Pastiche** (Cacavas) Gr. 2.5

TENOR SAXOPHONE
04002822	**Allegro Scherzando** (Haydn) Gr. 2.5
04002823	**Allemande and Courante** (Froberger) Gr. 3
04002824	**Harlequin Dance** (Cacavas) Gr. 2
04002825	**Impressionistic Air** (Cacavas) Gr. 2
04002826	**Overture Petit** (Cacavas) Gr. 3
04002827	**Theme from Symphony No. 40** (Mozart) Gr. 3

TRUMPET
04002828	**Allegro Scherzando** (Haydn) Gr. 2.5
04002829	**Eine Kleine Nachtmusik** (Mozart) Gr. 3
04002830	**Overture Petit** (Cacavas) Gr. 3
04002831	**Triumphal March from Aïda** (Verdi) Gr. 3

F HORN
04002832	**Allegretto from Symphony No. 7** (Beethoven) Gr. 2
04002833	**Danse Ancienne** (Cacavas) Gr. 2
04002834	**Poem** (Cacavas) Gr. 3
04002835	**Sarabande** (Corelli) Gr. 1.5
04002836	**Summer Pastiche** (Cacavas) Gr. 2.5

TROMBONE
04002837	**Allegretto from Symphony No. 7** (Beethoven) Gr. 1
04002838	**Minuet and Trio** (Bach) Gr. 2.5
04002839	**Overture Petit** (Cacavas) Gr. 3
04002840	**Sonatina** (Weber) Gr. 3
04002841	**Triumphal March from Aïda** (Verdi) Gr. 3

BARITONE B.C.
04002842	**Liebestraum** (Liszt) Gr. 2
04002843	**Minuet and Trio** (Bach) Gr. 2.5
04002844	**Poem** (Cacavas) Gr. 3
04002845	**Sonatina** (Weber) Gr. 3

BARITONE T.C.
04002846	**Allegro Scherzando** (Haydn) Gr. 2.5
04002847	**Eine Kleine Nachtmusik** (Mozart) Gr. 3
04002848	**Overture Petit** (Cacavas) Gr. 3
04002849	**Triumphal March from Aïda** (Verdi) Gr. 2

VIOLIN
04002850	**Danse Ancienne** (Cacavas) Gr. 2
04002851	**Impressionistic Air** (Cacavas) Gr. 2
04002852	**Minuet and Trio** (Bach) Gr. 2.5
04002853	**Summer Pastiche** (Cacavas) Gr. 2.5
04002854	**Symphony No. 40 (Theme)** (Mozart) Gr. 3

CELLO
04002855	**Jesu, Joy of Man's Desiring** (Bach) Gr. 2.5
04002856	**Liebestraum** (Liszt) Gr. 2
04002857	**Minuet and Trio** (Bach) Gr. 2.5
04002858	**Poem** (Cacavas) Gr. 3

FRENCH HORN SOLOS with Piano Accompaniment

HL04477710	Allerseelen, Op. 10 No. 8 (R. Strauss/Voxman)	*Grade 2.5*
HL04477711	Ballade (Ostransky)	*Grade 1.5*
HL04477717	Meadowland (traditional/Hurrell)	*Grade 2*
HL04477719	Romance, Op. 36 (Saint-Saens/Voxman)	*Grade 3*
HL04477720	Romanze from Concerto No. 3 (Mozart/Voxman)	*Grade 3*
HL04477721	Sarabanda and Gavotta (Corelli/Hurrell)	*Grade 3*
HL04477725	Third Movement from Concerto No. 2 (Mozart/Voxman)	*Grade 4*

BRASS ENSEMBLES

HL04479707	Aeolian Suite (horn quartet) (Ostransky)	*Grade 3*
HL04479733	Aria and Minuet (brass quintet) (Scarlatti/arr. Johnson)	*Grade 3*
HL04479726	Bach Chorales for Brass Quartet (Johnson)	*Grade 2*
HL04479728	Chaconne in D Minor (brass quartet) (Long)	*Grade 4*
HL04479744	Chorale and March (brass sextet) (Beethoven/Lotzenhiser)	*Grade 3*
HL04477699	Fanfare Prelude (brass trio, accomp.) (Koepke)	*Grade 2*
HL04479746	Four Chorales for Brass Sextet (Bach/Johnson)	*Grade 2*
HL04479730	Gavotte from Sonata No. 6 (brass quartet) (Bach/Irons)	*Grade 2*
HL04479736	If Thou Be Near (brass quintet) (Bach/Beeler)	*Grade 3*
HL04479738	Quintet in B Minor – Third Movement (Ewald/Voxman)	*Grade 5*
HL04477695	Serenade (brass duet, accomp.) (Koepke)	*Grade 2*
HL04479741	Sonata No. 27 (brass quintet) (Pezel/Brown)	*Grade 2*
HL04479863	Spanish Dance No. 4 (brass choir) (Moszkowski/Holmes)	*Grade 4*
HL04477696	Spring Odyssey (brass duet, accomp.) (Johnson)	*Grade 3*
HL04479749	Suite for Brass Sextet (Ostransky)	*Grade 3*
HL04479752	Trumpet Tune and Air (brass sextet) (Purcell/Brown)	*Grade 2*
HL04479859	Two Intradas (brass sextet) (Franck/Long)	*Grade 2*
HL04479860	Woodland Sketches (brass choir) (MacDowell/Johnson)	*Grade 2*